BITE BOOKS

A Bite-Sized Public Affairs Book

Narendra Modi

The Yogi of Populism

by

Mihir Bose

Cover by
Dean Stockton

Published by Bite-Sized Books Ltd 2021
©Bite-Sized Books Ltd

BITE-SIZED BOOKS

Bite-Sized Books Ltd Cleeve Road, Goring RG8 9BJ UK
information@bite-sizedbooks.com

Registered in the UK. Company Registration No: 9395379

ISBN: 9798709690790

The moral right of Mihir Bose to be identified as the author of this work has been asserted by him in accordance with the Copyright, Designs and Patents
Act 1988

Although the publisher, editors and authors have used reasonable care in preparing this book, the information it contains is distributed as is and without warranties of any kind. This book is not intended as legal, financial, social or technical advice and not all recommendations may be suitable for your situation. Professional advisors should be consulted as needed. Neither the publisher nor the author shall be liable for any costs, expenses or damages resulting from use of or reliance on the information contained in this book.

Reviews of the book

Ben Fenton, former Daily Telegraph and Financial Times

Brimming with Bose's intimate knowledge of his homeland, this brief description of the Indian prime minister's rise from tea-seller to premier tells new readers all they need to know about what we might call the Modi Operandus.

Bose explains in flowing prose how Narendra Modi exploited dormant anti-secularism among India's Hindu majority and reversed its multicultural trends. Modi's brand of populism predates Trump or Brexit or Bolsanaro. As such, it is a template for the creation of a vision of a nation where economic growth is not quite what it seems and history has been rewritten to suit a Hindu-centric view of the whole world.

Using vignettes like Modi's building the world's highest statue to honour a political idol, Bose paints an elegantly candid picture of a man who stands tall in the new gallery of strongmen rulers.

David Smith, Economics Editor Sunday Times

This is a fascinating and original take on one of the most interesting political leaders of our age.

Contents

Mihir Bose — 2
Preface — 4
Chapter 1 — 6
  Real Tears and Pretend Tears
Chapter 2 — 9
  Mandir Politics
Chapter 3 — 15
  Real Tears and Pretend Tears
Chapter 4 — 19
  Making India Whole
Chapter 5 — 23
  Stealing the Opposition's Jewel
Chapter 6 — 32
  Rewriting History
Chapter 7 — 37
  Dethroning the Lutyens Elite
Chapter 8 — 43
  Modi the Missionary
Chapter 9 — 48
  Modi's Other Cycle
Chapter 10 — 54
  The 56-inch Teflon Man

Mihir Bose

Mihir Bose, who was born in India but has lived in the UK for half a century, is an award-winning journalist and author.

He writes and broadcasts on social and historical issues as well as sport for a range of outlets including the BBC, the Financial Times, Evening Standard and Irish Times. He has written more than 30 books and his most recent publication is *Lion and Lamb, a Portrait of British Moral Duality*. His books range from a look at how India has evolved since Independence, the only narrative history of Bollywood, biographies of Michael Grade, the Indian nationalist Subhas Bose, and a study of the Aga Khans.

Mihir was the BBC's first Sports Editor, and the first non-white to be a BBC editor. He covered all BBC outlets including the flagship Ten O'clock News, the Today programme, Five Live and the website. He moved to the BBC after 12 years at the Daily Telegraph where he was the chief sports news correspondent but also wrote on other issues including race, immigration, and social and cultural issues. Before that he worked for the Sunday Times for 20 years. He has contributed to nearly all the major UK newspapers and presented programmes for radio and television and has edited several business publications.

Mihir was awarded an honorary doctorate from Loughborough University for his outstanding contribution to journalism and the promotion of equality. He has won several awards: business columnist of the year, sports news reporter of the year, sports story of the year and Silver Jubilee Literary award for his *History of Indian Cricket*.

Mihir lives in west London with his wife.

Mihir is a former chairman of the Reform Club and has recently been appointed to the Blue Plaques selection committee of English Heritage.

Preface

The idea of Narendra Modi providing the template for Donald Trump and Boris Johnson to seize power may sound absurd. What can the Prime Minister of a developing country, who leads a hard right Hindu party, have to teach two leaders of sophisticated rich countries which pride themselves on being long-established democracies?

The British never fail to remind the world that they have the mother of Parliaments and the Magna Carta plotted the route to democracy back in the 13th century when the rest of the world was run by people claiming to be divine kings. But while Britain and America may be longer established democracies India is the world's largest democracy and Modi's playbook for winning elections has provided a model for both Trump and Johnson.

The Modi template says to win power you must convince enough people that they have lost their country. That they need to do something very radical if they are to regain their country.

This is such an emotive call that it can galvanise people even when there is no merit whatsoever in the argument. Modi's success came in the Indian general elections of 2014 which, contrary to the predictions of all the pollsters, and the views of India's chattering classes, saw his Bharatiya Janata Party sweep to victory with a two-thirds majority. Before Modi the BJP had been a regional party which had only been in power at the federal level as part of a messy Indian coalition. Now Modi had crushed the Congress, the traditional ruling party of the country.

Two years later both Trump and Johnson did the same. Trump winning the Republican nomination when everyone thought his candidacy was a joke and then the Presidency by defeating the pollsters' favourite Hilary Clinton. Of course, the Trump victory reflected the curious electoral college system Americans use to elect their President. In other countries with Presidential systems Clinton would have become President as she won the popular vote by nearly three million.

Johnson, similarly, defied pollsters and opinion makers, masterminding the referendum victory that decided Britain should leave the European Union. Narrow as the victory margin was its appeal to people who felt they had been dispossessed cannot be denied.

Both Trump and Johnson campaigned on slogans which echoed the one used by Modi two years earlier. Trump argued that the elite, which included what he called the fake media and, in particular, the Washington swamp, had stolen the country from the real people of America and vowed to make America great again. Johnson's cry was that by leaving the EU Britain would take back control and regain sovereignty. Membership of the EU meant, he argued, Britain was a vassal state.

India may be very different to the US and the UK but we need to study Modi and how he secured power and continues to dominate Indian politics to see how populists can emerge. Modi, who likes yoga and has persuaded the UN to have a world yoga day, can claim to be the yogi of world populism providing yogic asanas that all populists can copy.

Chapter 1

Real Tears and Pretend Tears

In November 1981 I flew into Bombay, as the city was then called and where I had grown up, to cover the England-India Test series. My drive from the airport to my parents flat in south Mumbai, where I had lived for the first 21 years of my life before coming to Britain, took me over the Kemp's Corner flyover. I have driven over the flyover many times but every time I do I feel a sense of excitement.

For me the construction of the flyover marks a symbolic moment in the history of the city I feel most at home in India. It was the second flyover to be built in Bombay and in the 1960s it had made us feel that finally the city could be compared to London and other great western metropolises. But that morning as I sped past the flyover I noticed a curious graffiti on its wall. It read: "Mrs Gandhi save the Hindus".

I could not understand what this meant. Why should Indira Gandhi, then the Prime Minister, have to save the Hindus? Who was threatening them? They were the majority in the country and, while India was a secular republic, Hindus dominated the government, bureaucracy, business, judiciary, media, Bollywood, sport and almost all other areas of public life. I dismissed it as the work of some crank seeking publicity.

It is only in the 21st century that the real meaning behind that graffiti has emerged. What that cry for help articulated was the feeling of some Hindus that, despite being in the majority, they had lost their country and they needed a Prime Minister in

Delhi who would get their country back. Such cries are not unique to India and have been heard in other countries.

It is the cry of those who feel dispossessed. It was heard during the Brexit referendum in Britain and in America during the 2016 election. The tears may be fake as they were in India but as the referendum in Britain and Trump's emergence as President showed, such a cry of help however synthetic can bestow on those who know how to exploit it very real political power. We need to understand it if we are to explain why Narendra Modi now dominates Indian politics having won two general elections with thumping majorities, decimating the Congress, which led India to freedom and until Modi emerged was the natural party of government, and dramatically recast Indian politics.

The key to Modi's success is that he has drawn on this great reservoir of Hindu angst about the world they have lost and combined it with claiming to bring prosperity to India summed up in his 2014 election winning slogan of "*Acche Din Aane Waley Hain*", "Good days are coming". What may be called Modi's twin strategy of attending to the Hindu business and also the business of lifting millions of Indians from poverty.

Many who support him do so hoping he will attend to the Hindu business while many others have no time for his Hindu business but want him to attend to the business of making money. It was best put to me by Ajit Gulabchand, an old school friend of mine and a very successful businessman. For him what makes Modi important and crucial for India's progress is that he is just the business-friendly Prime Minister he has always wanted. "Fundamentally you have in Narendra Modi a very natural right-winger. I am not talking in terms of the Hindu business; I am talking of economics."

This may sound not very different from Trump who also worked on a twin track strategy of promising to make Americans more prosperous and keep immigrants out but while Trump did not conceal what he was going to do about immigrants Modi, while laying much stress on the money making business part of his strategy, has never openly advertised what he was going to do on the Hindu business front. But that is because unlike Trump he did not need to.

Many Americans had long been hostile to immigration from Mexico and other parts of the Hispanic world but until Trump gave them a catchy slogan they could all mouth there was nothing they could rally round. Modi's Hindu supporters had such a rallying call long before Modi emerged as a political leader and it was uncannily similar to what Trump and his supporters yelled when he campaigned for the Presidency in 2016. Trump's cry was Build the Wall, the Hindu slogan was Build the Mandir, temple. It is impossible to understand the rise of Modi without studying the revolutionary change the slogan has brought to Indian politics.

Mandir politics has completely reshaped the Indian political landscape and laid the groundwork for Modi to work his political magic and become the supreme political leader of his time.

Chapter 2

Mandir Politics

The Mandir Hindus wanted built was on a plot of land in Ayodhya, a holy city in the Indian state of Uttar Pradesh. Devout Hindus believe Lord Rama, one of the most revered of Hindu gods, was born at the site, that there had been a temple there which was destroyed on the orders of Babar, the first Mughal emperor and Babri Masjid, a mosque, built in its place.

It summed up the way many Hindus have demonised the Muslims: predatory conquerors who looted their land, destroyed Hindu temples and raped their women. The claim on Babri Masjid was fiercely contested by the Muslims. The dispute dates back to the days of the British Raj but took centre stage in Indian politics when in 1990 L. K. Advani, a mentor of Modi and then deputy leader of Modi's Bharatiya Janata Party, organised a *rath yathra*, chariot ride, his chariot being a Toyota van which had been modified to look like a *rath*, on a 6,000-mile journey through nine Indian states to Ayodhya.

His demand was that a temple be built on that site. Two years later Hindu mobs, helped by wretched policing by the local Uttar Pradesh government run by the BJP, demolished the Babri Masjid. Never before in Indian history had a mosque been pulled down. It led to religious violence between Hindus and Muslims in several states, hundreds died with the brunt of the violence in Mumbai where 800 people were killed, two thirds of them Muslims. Advani and the other BJP leaders played a curious role as the mosque was pulled down. Advani had been in Ayodhya that day calling for a temple to be built but had also tried to stop the mosque being demolished and would go on to publicly express regret. Other BJP leaders distanced themselves from the sacrilege and the common political view then was that in secular India such an outrage could not be tolerated and the mosque would be rebuilt.

Modi had visited the site in 1991 when the Babri Masjid was still there, and Modi was an unknown. He had vowed that he would not return until work on the temple had begun. Now, nearly three decades later, Modi has so transformed the political landscape that in August 2020 he returned to Ayodhya to lay the foundation stone for the new temple with no talk of rebuilding Babri Masjid.

Modi was helped by the Indian Supreme Court which, after the sort of endless legal wrangling that Indians much enjoy, finally ruled in 2019 that the site was government property and should be handed over to a trust for a temple to be built with another site given for a mosque. Modi was quick to seize the invitation.

On 5 August 2020 Modi arrived in Ayodhya displaying all the power of the Indian state. Dressed in a top of glimmering Indian kurta in bright yellow and wearing a pristine white dhoti he sat on the floor wearing a mask and offered garlands and prayers to the deity to the sound of conch shells blown by priests in saffron robes. At the temple site a 40kg silver foundation stone was placed in the ground.

Calling the temple foundation laying ceremony, the "dawn of a new era" he said that "India is emotional as decades of wait has ended. For years, our Ram Lalla [the infant Lord Ram] lived beneath a tent; now he will reside in a grand temple."

Modi likes grand imposing architecture. And grand it will be with five domes, and clusters of columns, which will reach a height of 50 metres. It is timed to finish in 2024, ideal for Modi as this would be just before India goes to the polls and Modi seeks to win three successive elections. This has only been done once before in Indian history and that by the man who was India's first Prime Minister Jawaharlal Nehru, who stood for everything Modi hates, and would have been appalled by a Prime Minister of India laying the foundation for the temple.

How much Modi has changed India can be judged by how Nehru reacted to another demand by Hindus for a temple destroyed by Muslim invaders to be rebuilt. This was the temple in Somnath in the state of Gujarat where Modi comes from and whose chief minister he was for twelve years.

The temple had been destroyed by the Muslim Afghan ruler Mahmud Ghazni, who invaded India some seventeen times between 1000 and 1028, making these expeditions of plunder and loot something like his annual winter sport. On his 16th invasion he targeted the Somnath temple on the coast of Gujarat. Having vanquished the Hindu army, the Sultan entered the temple. He was so outraged by the gigantic idol he saw that he struck it with his iron mace, breaking the nose. The Brahmin priests offered him millions to spare their god and his advisers suggested he should accept. But Mahmud Ghazni, a devout Muslim, was a breaker of idols. As one historian put it, "At the next blow, the belly of the idol burst open: and forth issued a vast treasure of diamonds, rubies and pearls; rewarding the holy perseverance of Mahmud and explaining the devout liberality of the Brahmins."

For many Hindus the destruction of the temple is the Hindu equivalent of the destruction of the second temple of the Jews. Soon after independence there was a move to rebuild Somnath with one of Nehru's ministers saying that "I can assure you that the "collective sub-conscious" of India today is happier with the scheme of reconstruction of Somnath sponsored by the government of India than with many other things that we have done and are doing."

In fact, the restoration was funded by private doners but India's first President, Rajendra Prasad, inaugurated the rebuilt temple giving the reconstruction a veneer of official approval. Nehru was appalled and advised Prasad not to go as he, to quote Nehru's official biographer Gopal, "regarded this as totally contrary to the concept of secularism." But while he did not stop Prasad from going he, as Gopal put it, "sought to make it clear his government had no part in the decision." Gopal saw Prasad's association with the rebuilding of Somnath as evidence that India's first President "was still prominent in the ranks of medievalism."

It is a measure of Modi's transformation of India that in 2020 nobody in India's political class, many of whom revere Nehru and want to oust Modi from power, challenged the laying of the foundation stone at Ayodhya let alone dared to call an Indian Prime Minister's presence at the temple foundation ceremony an act of medievalism. And this despite the fact that, in contrast to Somnath, a mosque had not been demolished to build the temple.

The most remarkable reaction was from Nehru's great granddaughter and general secretary of the Congress party, Priyanka Gandhi who welcomed it and signed off with a 'Jai Siya Ram' — hail Ram, an act which would have made Nehru cringe. As for Muslims they only hoped Hindus would not seek to destroy other mosques that Hindus claim have been built on sites where temples once stood.

What Modi has done is bring what was once considered anathema and ideas at the very fringes of Indian society centre stage and convert these ideas into a touchstone of Hindu identity, part of his party's core ideology Hindutva, which can broadly be translated as the hegemony of the Hindu way of life, which all Indians whatever their faith must accept.

Modi's supporters argue that this should come as no surprise to people in the west. After all Britain considers itself secular yet the monarch is the head of the church, Britain sees itself as a Christian country and all state functions have a religious element to it and are often held in an Anglican church. A church of England priest is chaplain to the Speaker of the House of Commons and officiates at services held at the Palace of Westminster. Twenty-six bishops of the Church of England are members of the House of Lords. In America despite the much advertised separation of church and state, sessions of the US Congress commence and close with the chaplain saying Christian prayers. One of the most striking scenes of the US Congress session, held after the insurrection by Trump supporters, to ratify the electoral college vote in the 2020 Presidential election was to see the vice-President, who was presiding over it, call on the chaplain of the senate to say a few words to close the session. It would be inconceivable for a Hindu priest to perform anything similar in the Lok Sabha, India's House of Commons.

In the Indian republic that was founded after it won its freedom from the British, secularism has always had a very different meaning. It means the state has no religion, there are no religious ceremonies at state functions and for almost seventy years it would have been considered anathema in secular India for a Prime Minister to lay the foundation stone of a temple. That would have been seen as going against the letter and spirit of India's secular constitution and showing a woeful and total disregard for the principles that guided India's founding fathers.

Now Modi's political opponents not only dare not voice such views for fear of alienating many of their fellow Hindus but are so keen not to appear to be out of step with majority sentiment that they eagerly advertise that they are Hindus. In 2018 Shashi Tharoor, a Congress MP and one of Modi's most vocal critics, wrote a book called *Why I am a Hindu*. Before Modi recast Indian politics such an advertisement of Hindu credentials by a Congressman would have classified him as a communalist , the Indian word for a religious bigot and a term which is equivalent to calling somebody racist in the west.

His party leader, Rahul Gandhi, great-grandson of Nehru, has gone even further making a great show of being a devout Hindu wearing a 'janeu' (sacred thread of Brahmins) and making temple visits. For Rahul Gandhi this is particularly important for while the Nehru family are Brahmins, his grandmother married a Parsi, and he is the son of an Italian Catholic mother. Against such a background it is all the more important in Modi's India to stress his Hindu heritage.

Chapter 3

The Two Faces of Modi

But even as Modi has attended to the Hindu business, what has set him apart from Trump and many other demagogues is that he does not openly attack Muslims. Observe the contrast with Trump. Trump started his primary campaign for the Republican nomination in 2016 by calling Mexican immigrants, drug dealers, criminals and rapists. Modi has never categorised Muslims in that fashion. He does not talk about what Hindutva means to him personally but told Nilanjan Mukhopadhay, one of his biographers, "Forget the literal meaning - in essence it means well-being of all without distinctions of sect, or of one geographical area."

For some opponents this is a mask he wears, confident that he has willing minions to spearhead the anti-Muslim campaign and Modi is careful to make sure these minions are in positions of authority. This balancing of Hindu business with the business of making Indians better off has always been a feature of Modi's politics and was evident from his early days as chief minister of Gujarat. Back in 2002, a few months after he had taken power in the state, and when few would have seen him as a man capable of becoming Prime Minister of India, there were horrific killings of Muslims in the state.

A train carrying Hindu pilgrims was torched by Muslims with fifty-nine people including twenty-six women and twelve children burnt. The pilgrims were returning from visiting Ayodhya where they had offered prayers at the Ram site and expressed their desire for the Ram temple to be rebuilt. Their slaughter by Muslims was seen as revenge for the destruction of the Babri Masjid and send shock waves through the Hindu community in Gujarat.

Their retaliation against Muslims was ferocious and in the violence that followed more than a thousand were killed, most of them Muslims. The charge against Modi was he did nothing, just let them die. But while some politicians, including members of both the BJP and the Congress, were convicted and jailed nothing was ever proven against Modi.

The Special Investigations Team, SIT, set up by the Indian Supreme Court, to which Modi gave evidence, concluded, that while the evidence he gave "possibly indicates his discriminatory attitude", "no criminal case is made out against Narendra Modi". Modi had called out the army "on time to contain the communal violence." One allegation made against Modi was he had told senior police officers "to allow Hindus to vent their anger". The SIT report found there was no truth to this allegation.

However, Modi has never apologised for what happened or condemned it and for a man who likes to hear his own voice this is one subject he does not like talking about. When Lance Price the former Blair adviser, who wrote a book on Modi, asked him about it he rebuffed him saying he had spoken enough on the subject and Price could read the Supreme Court judgement.

The 2014 BJP manifesto neatly illustrated how Modi can sit astride both the Hindu cycle and the business cycle. In the Cultural Heritage section, it committed itself to building the temple, defending Hindu culture, cleaning up the Ganges, which Hindus call Ma Ganga, Mother Ganges signifying its status as its holy river, protect cows and promote Indian languages.

However, Muslims were not forgotten but they were offered the business carrot. "It is unfortunate that even after several decades of independence, a large section of the minority and especially Muslim community continues to be stymied in poverty. Modern India must be a nation of equal opportunity. BJP is committed to ensure that all communities are equal partners in India's progress, as we believe India cannot progress if any segment of Indians is left behind."

Yet when in 2017 BJP contested the state elections in Uttar Pradesh, India's largest state, despite 16 per cent of the population being Muslim it did not field a single Muslim candidate. When BJP won Modi appointed Yogi Adityanath, who wears the full saffron robes of Hindu priests, has never concealed his anti-Muslim views, and who was being investigated for inciting religious hatred and rioting among other offences, as chief minister. Soon the Yogi was at work dealing with what he called people who illegally stored beef in their homes.

On the face of it this sounds just the thing a reasonable government would do, the state having many unlicensed butchers and abattoirs. But in singling out the meat industry the Yogi was targeting Muslims. He did not have to broadcast it as this was known to everybody. The cow is sacred to Hindus, very few Hindus eat beef, even fewer would be prepared to kill a cow. The meat industry is dominated by Muslims and as the writer Aatish Taseer put it, "the politician-priest knew that he was in effect leading an attack on Muslim business with shades of Kistallnacht".

The yogi had for good measure exhorted his followers to kill ten Muslims for every Hindu killed. Modi for all his claims to revolutionise Indian business followed through by putting such onerous new rules on purchases of cattle that it created havoc in the booming beef-exporting business. But perhaps Modi's ability to outdo Janus and look both ways was best exemplified when his government suddenly decided to abrogate article 370 of the Indian constitution.

Chapter 4

Making India Whole

Just as every American child knows about the second amendment of the US constitution which allows Americans to bear arms everybody in India knows about article 370. This has given the province of Kashmir a special status in India. While it is part of the union and India also claims the part of Kashmir that is ruled by Pakistan calling it Pakistan Occupied Kashmir, the Indian constitution gave the state a unique status. Until August 2019 Kashmir had a separate constitution, a state flag and autonomy over the internal administration of the state which meant Indians from other states could not go and live there or work there without the permission of the Kashmir government.

Kashmir is a touchstone for Indians. India has fought three wars over Kashmir with Pakistan. The line of control that divides the Indian part of the state from the Pakistan part has seen numerous firings. It is the one issue that fiercely divides the two countries. Kashmir is the only Muslim majority state in India and India's founding fathers always saw Kashmir being part of India as proof that, unlike Pakistan which was created as a confessional state because Muslims of the subcontinent claimed they needed a state of their own and could not be a minority in a country dominated by Hindus, Kashmir showed that India could be a secular country home to people of all faiths and beliefs.

For years India has struggled to deal with the insurgents in Kashmir who want to free the state from what they see as an

Indian yoke and either have an independent state on the style of Switzerland or join Pakistan. This has required the deployment of the Indian army and while India blames Pakistan for fomenting trouble and arming the militants many others see India acting like a colonial power using repressive measures comparable to the ones the British Raj inflicted on Indians. The three decades of agitation between Kashmiri militants and the Indian Army has claimed an estimated 40,000 lives.

Since India became independent a constant demand of the various parties that have claimed to represent the Hindus is that article 370 be revoked. They accuse successive governments of being weak and spineless in dealing with what they categorise as Pakistan directed terrorism. To revoke Article 370 has also been part of BJP manifestoes long before Modi was a political force. But despite Modi's thumping majority nobody expected this manifesto pledge to be fulfilled.

Then in August 2019, three months after winning a second term with a landslide election victory, Modi suddenly granted their wish. A resolution was passed in both houses of India's parliament by a two thirds majority suspending article 370 and making all the provisions of the Indian constitution applicable to Jammu and Kashmir. A Presidential Order was issued implementing the resolution.

The state was split into two union territories.

Modi's government knew revoking article 370 would prompt a furious response amongst Kashmiris and the state was put under a draconian lockdown, key leaders jailed, communications blocked, and thousands of troops patrolled the streets. It was only in January 2021 that high-speed mobile internet connection was restored in Kashmir with India earning the dubious distinction of having imposed the longest blackout in any democracy. Kashmiris have called the 18-month blackout "digital apartheid" and claimed it has decimated the economy of the state.

It has been estimated by the Kashmiri Chamber of Commerce that the state, whose beauty has always attracted a lot of visitors, in the 50s and 60s it was the favourite location for Bollywood movies, lost £1.85 billion as tourism and agriculture was not able to function. Imran Khan, the Prime Minister of Pakistan, accused India of "ethnic cleansing and genocide" but Modi justified it as a vital step for the good of the Kashmiris as this would bring prosperity with investors from the rest of the country finally able to invest in the state.

Modi, aware how popular this move would be with his base, shrewdly calculated that the international opprobrium could be contained. He has not been proven wrong. So, while both US Congressmen and British MPs were critical of India it was significant that the response from both governments was much more muted.

In the House of Commons, the debate about Kashmir was more revealing about internal British politics than what was happening in that province. It was noticeable that the sharpest comments about the Indian action came not from the Conservatives but from Labour with the Labour front bench very critical of India. Many of them are from constituencies which have a large population from Mirpur in Pakistan Kashmir and were aware of how concerned their constituents were about what the Indians had done in Kashmir. In contrast Conservatives, who do not have quite so many Mirpuris in their constituencies, were less critical and even saw some merit in the Indian action with one mentioning it would mean that discrimination against women in Kashmir, reflecting the attitude to women in a Muslim majority state, would now end.

Very significantly Dominic Raab, the foreign secretary, was very careful to make no critical comments about India. For Modi this was a small price to be paid for fulfilling a long-felt demand of his Hindu base just as it was with the construction of the temple. It also meant that he could now right what Modi and many in his party see as a great historical wrong and in the process undo the legacy of Nehru, Modi and BJP's bête noire. It also helps to promote another leader of the Indian freedom movement, Sardar Vallabhbhai Patel. He was known as the Iron Man of Indian politics and for Modi, who would love to be seen as India's present day Iron Man, Patel is the ideal hero and a wonderful stick with which to strike against Nehru and what he sees as Nehru's dreadful legacy.

Chapter 5

Stealing the Opposition's Jewel

Patel is a little-known figure outside India but he was a colossal figure in the Indian freedom movement. A Middle Temple lawyer Patel was Gandhi's right-hand man who ran the Congress party political machine. It was Gandhi who gave him the title Sardar, a title that means leader and is often given to the man who organises gangs of workers at various workplaces.

A ruthless political operator he made sure the Congress never strayed from what Gandhi wanted. Gandhi may have anointed Nehru as his chosen successor but while Nehru was the charismatic leader who could make wonderful speeches that wooed the masses he was a poor organiser. In contrast Patel was the political operator with a masterful control over the Congress party machine which delivered Congress successes and made sure opponents were ground to dust.

When India became independent Patel became deputy Prime Minister and played a crucial role in creating the independent Indian nation that emerged. Contrary to popular myth the British did not rule all of India. Some 45 per cent of the total area of the country (excluding Burma and Sind) and about 23 per cent of the population was under the control of Indian princes many of whom had helped the British secure India. The British Foreign Office recognised about 680 native states. These states had internal autonomy and the criminal law of British India did not extend to the princely states nor did the railways the British had brought to India. The bigger princely states, like Hyderabad, which was bigger than France, could even impose the death penalty, although not on Europeans. Hyderabad also had its own currency.

The British saw these princely states as essential to their rule in India. The rulers were willing collaborators of the Raj providing men to fight for the British and generous funds during both the world wars. Many of them were also badly governed and the British could always point to these states to justify their rule in India arguing that Indian rule of the princely states showed how incompetent Indians were in ruling their country.

In 1947 as the British left India these princely states were given three options: they could join India, join Pakistan or become independent. The British were sure that the Indians would not manage to integrate the princely states. Patel proved them wrong demanding from Lord Mountbatten, the last Viceroy, that the "apples", as he called the princely states, be delivered to him by the British. He masterminded the integration of these very diverse princely states but Kashmir eluded him. But for Modi and his followers this was not Patel's fault but the result of Nehru's incompetence, his possible love for an English woman, and represents an indictment of his misguided, secular, policies. Had Patel been in charge, they argue, there would have been no Kashmir problem.

But with Kashmir being one of the most curious legacies of the British Raj, it was never going to be easy to make it part of India. The largely Muslim state had been sold to a Hindu warlord by the British in the 19th century. The Hindu rulers of Kashmir illustrated the British argument that Indians could not govern, and their Muslims subjects often rose in revolts which were brutally put down.

Both Pakistan and India wanted Kashmir; the prince, Hari Singh, who was an effete, ineffectual and debauched ruler, dithered, hoping to keep Kashmir independent. A month after India became free and Pakistan was formed the Pakistanis sent tribal militia and soldiers in civilian clothes to annex the state. Hari Singh desperately trying to save his kingdom called for Indian help, signed the Instrument of Accession, ceding Jammu and Kashmir to India, Jammu being the Hindu majority part of the state. Indian troops arrived by air and saved Srinagar the capital falling to the Pakistani forces.

And this is where Modi's supporters see Nehru's actions as nothing short of criminal. Nehru did not force the Pakistani forces entirely out of Kashmir. Pakistan held on to part of the state and Gilgit and Baltistan. Nehru also allowed himself to be guided by Lord Mountbatten, who had become Governor General of India, and whose wife, Edwina, was, it is generally believed, Nehru's lover. He accepted Mountbatten's proposal that India would hold a plebiscite after law and order was imposed. Worse still he agreed to Mountbatten's suggestion and took the Kashmir issue to the United Nations. Patel had opposed going to the UN. Nehru overruled him.

By internationalising the issue Nehru tied a noose round India's neck from which it has never been able to escape. This has seen the Security Council holding endless debates over Kashmir and India requiring the Russian veto to prevent the Security Council passing resolutions which would make Indian rule in Kashmir even more difficult.

Modi and his supporters contrast the mess they claim Nehru made with Kashmir with how Patel handled Hyderabad and made sure it was integrated into India. Hyderabad was the mirror image of Kashmir, its Muslim ruler the Nizam, ruling over a largely Hindu state. The Nizam did not want to be part of India and, despite the fact that it is in the south surrounded by Indian territory and far from Pakistan, tried hard to join the Muslim state Mohammed Ali Jinnah had created.

The British, who were keen on Pakistan, and did not believe India would survive, encouraged the Nizam.. Patel sent in the Indian Army and crushed the rebellion. Soon after Patel accompanied by Chaudhuri, the Indian general in charge of what the Indians, borrowing the language the British had often used, called "police action", and Vidya Shankar, his ICS trained private secretary, flew down to Hyderabad and met the Nizam of Hyderabad.

At the height of the conflict the Nizam had written a verse in which he had praised the defeat of the conch and the sacred thread, two objects with great religious significance for the Hindus. Patel was determined to remind him of his anti-Hindu utterances. At Patel's command Shankar recited the verse, and the abject Nizam apologised. It showed how, unlike Nehru, Patel was not afraid to proclaim that he was a Hindu or take to task anyone who defamed the religion.

Modi had expressed his admiration for Patel as soon as he became Gujarat chief minister, making the most of the fact that Patel was also from Gujarat. He started a project to build a bronze and iron state of Patel in the state, the so-called Statue of Unity. It was inaugurated in 2018 and at 182 metres is the tallest statue in the world and the second tallest monument in the world, second to the St. Louis Arc. Its cost, an estimated $430 million, is as much as Gujarat spends on women's safety, and twice its budget for promoting education for girls. The statue not only honours Patel but also represents an essential part of Modi's character, for as an aide put it "With Modi everything has to be the biggest, the boldest or the best".

Not content with that Modi also renamed Ahmedabad's cricket stadium after Patel. As chief minister he was also President of the Gujarat cricket association and initially suggested minor upgrades to the stadium then known as the Gujarat stadium. But soon after winning the 2014 national election he proposed it be rebuilt and having heard the Melbourne Cricket Ground was the largest in the world with a capacity of 100,000 ordered the new stadium to able to seat 110,000.

In February 2020 with the stadium now called the Sardar Patel Stadium this is where Modi hosted Trump when he visited India.

Promoting Patel has been a constant theme of Modi's prime ministership. Months after he became Prime Minister he named 31 October Rashtriya Ekta Divas, National Unity Day, to mark Patel's birthday.

The choice of 31 October 2014 as the first celebration of this new holiday seemed odd, as it marked 139 years since Patel was born, and a 139th birthday is not normally an occasion for celebration. But clearly Modi did not want to waste time to show his devotion to Patel.

This is where Modi's shrewdness as a political operator comes in. For in making Patel his hero Modi has cleverly stolen a man who was a jewel of the Congress party. Patel died three years after India won freedom and with the Nehru clan taking charge of the Congress party Patel has been written out of modern Indian history with the Congress party totally ignoring his contribution to India's freedom movement.

While Gandhi is revered as the father of the nation with his face on every Indian rupee and Nehru is lauded for creating the framework of modern India, Patel is hardly mentioned. Now suddenly the Congress find that their greatest opponent has claimed a man who, while he was alive, was integral to the Congress party. The Congress party was to wake up to this steal but by then Modi had bolted with the Congress stallion.

Realising what Modi was doing when, soon after his election as Prime Minister, he laid the foundation stone for Patel's statue the outgoing Congress Prime Minister Manmohan Singh remined everyone that Patel was a Congressman. Modi's response was classic. He said the statue was for everyone and that "we should not divide our legacy".

It is as if the Conservative party aware how treasured the NHS is would now claim Aneurin Bevan, the Labour minister who masterminded it, as one of their own. This, of course, would be absurd as Bevan once described the Conservatives as lower than vermin. Interestingly Patel considered Hindu fanatics as not much better and when in power dealt with them ruthlessly.

As Home Minister it fell to Patel to deal with the aftermath of Gandhi's assassination. The assassin, Nathuram Godse, was a Hindu fanatic and a member of the Hindu Mahasabha, the main Hindu party at the time of Indian independence, of which the BJP can be considered a heir. Patel banned the Mahasabha, had several of its members jailed and Godse was hanged. Godse had once belonged to the RSS, a voluntary organisation that claims it seeks to protect Hinduism but which its opponents see as a fascist organisation dedicated to making India a Hindu nation to which all minorities should be subservient. Patel banned the RSS.

Modi would rather draw a veil over that for he has been a member of the RSS since he was a boy and its leadership helped make sure that he would be the BJP candidate for Prime Ministership in the 2014 election. Patel would have been horrified that Modi's 2014 election victory gave encouragement for Godse's admirers to emerge from the woodwork. So much so that Sakshi Maharaj, a fairly prominent BJP MP, even went on television to call Godse "not anti-national" but "a patriot."

Here again we can see how craftily Modi plays such outbursts from his followers. Following outraged reaction to eulogising the man who killed the father of the nation Maharaj sheepishly backtracked saying, "I may have said something by mistake." The way Maharaj apologised suggested he did so under pressure from Modi. As for Patel's handling of the Hindu fanatics no reference is made by Modi or others in the BJP who have done so much to revive his name. This is an inconvenient truth that they would rather not know.

So keen are Modi's supporters to promote Patel that, a few years ago, Patel was honoured in the Houses of Parliament at an event organised by an Indian group many of them from Gujarat and whose admiration for Modi is not in doubt. The then Conservative Attorney General Dominic Grieve spoke glowingly about Patel.

It is just not Patel's Hinduism that appeals to Modi and his supporters. He has also argued that if Patel, not Nehru, had unfurled the Indian tricolour on the midnight of 15 August, 1947, "the country's fate and face would have been completely different."

The argument goes that Patel would have promoted free enterprise, business friendly policies instead of Nehru's socialism. This was so bureaucratic with government permission required for almost any enterprise that Indians dubbed it the "license permit Raj". There is no way of knowing this as the initial steps for government control of business was actually welcomed by many of India's most prominent businessmen.

But if in lauding Patel Modi is seeking to make the Congress party more of a marginal force in Indian politics the "Let us not forget the Sardar" campaign is also, of course, a "Get Nehru" campaign. This has given them licence to voice such anti-Nehru feelings that some of the BJP supporters have even indulged in wild fantasies about the origins of the Nehru family.

I was made very aware of this when visiting Anand Bhavan, the family home of the Nehrus, which used to be headquarters of the Congress party when it was fighting for India's freedom, and which the Nehrus gave to the nation. As school children from Allahabad were being shown around, I met a man who tried to convince me that Nehru was actually a Muslim. He pointed to a photograph on the wall of Nehru's grandfather: "Look at him. He is a Muslim who pretended to be a Hindu".

He also claimed that Feroze Gandhi, the Parsi who married Nehru's daughter Indira, was also a Muslim. He told me he had been given the name Feroze by Mahatma Gandhi to make him sound like a Parsi.

This has long been the stuff of internet bile, but to hear a man who seemed very reasonable utter such rubbish with absolute conviction in the very house where Nehru and Indira Gandhi had lived made me realise how some of the wider fringes that make up the Hindu base of Modi's party think. This is part of a larger mission of rewriting Indian history.

Chapter 6

Rewriting History

History can be lethal. In India it is even more so. Long before Modi, Hindu fanatics have been busy trying to rewrite history. Many years ago, at the height of Indira Gandhi's emergency, I met in a central Delhi restaurant P.N.Oak, who today would be called India's QAnon leader. He was a member of the Jan Sangh, the parent of the BJP.

With Indira Gandhi having imposed emergency rule Jan Sangh leaders were imprisoned and we met furtively not sure what might happen. He ran what he called the Institute for Rewriting Indian History. He claimed that the Taj Mahal had originally been a Hindu palace that the Muslims had appropriated and renamed. And that the Hindus had once had a world empire. The ancient Hindu empire, he claimed, had slipped out of their memory.

After further morsels of cakes were consumed he tried to correct this remarkable amnesia. The Coronation Stone, Oak claimed, was really the Hindu God Shiva's penis; Shrewsbury was an old Sanskrit name; England had been a colony of India.

When I asked how he could make such a claim he said, do you know why in Britain midnight marks the change of dates? Surely that is a very odd time to do that. The reason, he said, is because midnight GMT is 5.30 in the morning in India. For Hindus sunrise marks the start of the day, and when the Hindus had their world empire, as the sun rose the call would go out from the Ganges all over the world and the British, then under

Hindu colonial rule, would change their date, even though for them it was midnight.

In that Delhi restaurant it was easy to dismiss Oak as the sort of fantasist all countries have although even then some Indian newspapers reviewed Oak's books as if they were serious studies. But now more such fantasy theories can be heard in very respectable places.

Within weeks of Modi's election, an organisation in Leicester started seeking funds to make a programme to prove Oak's thesis on the Taj Mahal. In January 2015, at the Indian Science Congress in Mumbai Captain Anand Bodas, described how during the Vedic Age ancient Hindus had invented aviation technology, with planes flying from one planet to another and capable of mid-air stops.

Bodas explained, "There is official history and unofficial history." He went on, "Official history only noted that the Wright Brothers flew the first plane in 1903." But what made all this different from what Oak told me in Delhi while eating cake was that not only was this the first time in its 102 years that the Indian Science Congress had held a symposium on such a subject, but it was attended by Prakash Javadekar, the Environment Minister. His comment on Bodas's speech was, "Ancient Indian scientific theories were based on minute observations and logic. That wisdom must be recognised."

It must be said that Modi, unlike Trump who spun elaborate fantasies in trying to prove he had beaten Joe Biden, has never endorsed such fantasies but the fact his wider electoral base, just like that of Trump, believes in many such fantasies indicates how he is willing to encourage those who would want nothing better than the Modi government to rewrite history. And while he may not openly talk of rewriting history it is significant that he, like many of his followers, sees India's slave status as having lasted not the near-200 years of British rule, but going all the way back to the first raids of Mahmud of Ghazni at the start of the previous millennium: 1,200 years. The message here is clear. Muslims are not really part of India but just as foreign as the British were.

Even before Modi the rise of the BJP and other regional parties had seen the secular nature of the country under attack and the ability of Hindus and Muslims to live together put under strain. In Mumbai, the most cosmopolitan of Indian cities, where Hindus had lived side by side with Muslims for generations, but which is now ruled by a regional Hindu party, Muslims found they could no longer buy houses or flats where Hindus resided.

A great feature of Hinduism has been tolerance and helped by the fact that unlike the revealed religions of Judaism, Christianity and Islam, the Hindus do not have a book which sets out its beliefs, it has always been able to accommodate other religions. But now that tolerance is fraying. Militant Hindus have been on a long campaign controversially converting Muslims, Christians and other minorities to Hinduism and while this started before Modi came to power in Delhi there are now more such cases. However, many Hindus are in denial about this. As one Hindu put it to me, "There are no conversions. It is known as shuddhikaran, or homecoming. Nothing more than that. At the fringe many things happen. The conversions are not forcible." What he was saying was these minorities were originally Hindus, albeit several generations back, and the generous Hindus were welcoming this flock that had gone astray back home.

Modi's rise has also seen an increase in the violent reactions against what Hindus call "love jihad". This, in the militant

Hindu world, stands for Muslim men marrying Hindu women. This Hindu idea dates back to the 19th century when Hindutva groups claimed that the aim of Muslim men was to seduce Hindu women to convert them to Islam and produce children who will grow up as Muslims. Not only do they find this repugnant but see it as a way Muslims are trying to subvert the Hindu faith and make India a Muslim nation.

Under Modi's rule what was confined to the fringe has become part of the national political discourse with four states controlled by the BJP passing anti-conversion laws. The fact is interfaith marriages and religious conversions are relatively rare in India. In 2018 the National Investigation Agency conducted an inquiry into interfaith marriages in Kerala and found no evidence of coercion in any of the cases examined.

A similar investigation that was conducted in September 2020 in Kanpur, Uttar Pradesh, reached the same conclusion. But with the backing of the law these states have seen Hindu vigilante groups work with the police to break up interfaith marriages often putting innocent Muslim men and boys behind bars. Even when families support such marriages the police have stopped such weddings. The BJP leaders insist that their "anti-conversion" laws are not targeting any specific group and aim only to protect women from being "conned into interfaith marriages".

The Modi government's most controversial anti-Muslim step was taken when in December 2019 the Indian Parliament passed the Citizenship Amendment Bill which reduced the period for illegal immigrants to be eligible for Indian citizenship from eleven years to six years. However, to get this benefit the illegal immigrants had to be from six religious minority communities - Hindu, Sikh, Buddhist, Jain, Parsi and Christian – who had been forced to flee because of religious persecution from three named countries, Pakistan, Afghanistan or Bangladesh.

The exclusion of Muslims from that list, when in these countries certain Muslim sects also face persecution, was a glaring and a very deliberate omission. BJP opinion makers made no secret of their aims with R Jagannathan, editorial director of *Swarajya* magazine, writing that "the exclusion of Muslims from the ambit of the bill's coverage flows from the obvious reality that the three countries are Islamist ones, either as stated in their own constitutions, or because of the actions of militant Islamists, who target the minorities for conversion or harassment". But as the historian Mukul Kesavan put it this is a play with words, the bill is "couched in the language of refuge and seemingly directed at foreigners, but its main purpose is the delegitimisation of Muslims' citizenship."

Chapter 7

Dethroning the Luytens Elite

Modi's supporters argue that the criticism of Modi represents the anger of India's anglicised elite that cannot get over the fact that seventy years after independence Modi has finally displaced them from power. There is merit in the argument that while India will next year celebrate 75 years since the British departed many Indians have not been able to shed their colonial hangover.

Vidya Nanjundiah, a distinguished scientist and an old friend, describes how in the world of science recognition is assessed by how often westerners acclaim Indians and how often Indians succeed in getting their work published in western journals. To get their papers graded for assessment or promotion in a scientific career, the scientists have to say how many papers have been published in international journals, and how many in Indian journals. And according to Nanjundiah it is taken as a mark of not having quite made it if many, or even a substantial minority, of the papers are in Indian journals. In recent years the arrival of modern technology has seen the emergence of international journals which are often bogus but as Nanjudiah puts it "Anything that carries the *chappa,* stamp, of being outside the borders" gives prestige to the scientific paper even if it has not been peer reviewed.

Modi's election success was a strike against this elite on the part of the non-English-speaking Indians with language forming an important part of their campaign. Although the Indian constitution specified that Hindi would be the official language, this objective was discarded many decades ago putting English on an equal footing with Hindi and at the elite level English has maintained its hold on Indians. India's English-speaking elite are proud of having been educated in what is called English medium schools, many of which are run by Jesuits or other Christian missionaries, where English is the main language of instruction with Hindi just one of the many languages taught as an additional subject.

Many amongst this elite have also been educated abroad either in the UK or US. For decades this elite has mocked their fellow Indians who do not speak English well. Modi did not go to university and his schooling was in his native tongue of Gujarati but he can surprise visitors by his command of English. Lance Price preparing to interview Modi was told he did not speak English well but found that he spoke "perfectly clear and coherent English, only occasionally reverting to his native Gujarati". However, at public events not only in India but also abroad Modi always speaks in Hindi, determined to emphasise that he is a new Indian, not part of the old colonial elite. Here again he stands out as his predecessors would rarely have done that.

Modi has exulted in not being part of the English-educated elite, what many Indians call the brown sahibs. When during the 2014 election a Cambridge educated Congress politician wondered if India would ever elect a tea seller to be Prime Minister Modi used his jibe to demonstrate his love for and identification with the common Indian. He described how he had helped his father sell tea at the Vadnagar railway station, his home town, and later ran a tea stall with his brother near a bus terminus. "I used to sell tea and snacks to the soldiers", and to further demonstrate his love for India said he dreamt of being a soldier.

He emphasised this distinction by always calling Rahul Gandhi, the Congress party leader, "Shehzada". This was a double-edged sword. The word means a spoiled brat, but it is of Urdu origin, the language Muslims in India speak, and its Muslim connotation would not have been missed by his supporters.

Yet for a tea seller Modi has been quick to show his grasp of social media almost at the level of Trump having a huge twitter following of 64.9 million and nearly 46 million likes on Facebook. Just as Trump has used twitter to undermine what he alleges is fake news put out by mainstream US media so Modi has used it to challenge the traditional media and the chattering classes of India and set his own agenda.

During the 2014 election having assembled technologically savvy men he used his website assiduously, attracted young voters by taking part in a Google+ Hangout session and used 3D Hologram technology that pop stars had used on stage shows but was then unknown in Indian politics. Modi knew many of the voters he was targeting may be poor, but they were aware of modern technology and would be impressed with it.

But for a man who is so quick to identify with the Indian poor as Prime Minister he has been keen to advertise his sartorial flair. When he met the Obamas in the White House he changed his outfit reportedly three times upstaging Michelle Obama and sharp observers noted that on his dark blue jacket the name of Modi had been stitched a thousand times into the garment. It could now be called the Modi jacket replacing its traditional name of the Nehru jacket.

Modi has been reported to splash out on accessories, with his glasses said to be from Bvlgari, and has a Movado watch and a Mont Blanc pen. Modi has said he made his kurta by cutting the sleeves of his shirt and is not afraid to boast of his dress sense. "Yes , I like to dress up well and stay clean. God has gifted me the sense of mixing and matching colours. So, I imagine everything on my own. Since I'm God gifted I fit well in everything. I have no fashion designer but I'm happy to hear that I dress well."

In displacing the Congress, which is still part of the old English elite, Modi has been eager to demonstrate that the masses, who had been ignored for so long, could acquire elite status without being part of the English- educated upper-middle class.

Modi has characterised this as the Luytens clan, a reference to Edwin Luytens who designed New Delhi after the British decided to move the capital from Kolkata to Delhi. In December 2020 with India coping with the Coronavirus and farmers opposed to agricultural reforms of the Modi government besieging the city he announced plans to begin a £2bn overhaul of Delhi's grand complex of government buildings in a bid to cut India's links with its colonial past.

He laid the foundation stone for a new building to replace Parliament House, designed by Lutyens and his fellow English architect Herbert Baker and which is the home of India's houses of parliament.

Modi plans to have the new building opened by 2022 to mark the 75th anniversary of India's independence. It will form one of several to be rebuilt along Raj Path, a wide avenue designed by Lutyens, which extends from India Gate to the Presidential Palace.

Opponents see this as proving that Modi is a typical fascist leader more so as plans were firmed up in May 2020 just as India's coronavirus figures skyrocketed to the second-highest number of cases in the world. The Indian-born sculptor Anish Kapoor writing in the *Guardian* saw the redevelopment as

Modi's way of "cementing his legacy as the ruler-maker-builder of a new Hindu India" and "dismantling the Nehru legacy of a secular India".

But for Modi such criticism only reinforced his claim that this was the voice of the elite that he has displaced saying at the ground-breaking ceremony that this new parliament building will be a "symbol of a new and self-reliant India". He added: "The coming generations will be proud to see the new Parliament House built in independent India. During independence, forecasts were made that democracy will not be successful in India. Today we can say with pride that we have proved the naysayers wrong."

For Modi this is an important strike against the Lutyens elite which has always mocked the BJP. This has ranged from making fun of the members of the RSS, Modi's alma mater, for having grown men wearing flared khaki shorts, the RSS has since moved on to trousers, and being even more damming of the BJP's intellectual pretences. When under the first BJP-led coalition government of 1998 the party's economists made pronouncements the Indian-born Columbia University economist Jagdish Bhagwati quipped, "If they are economists, then I am a Bharata Natyam dancer!" Modi when elected in 2014 may have thought he could win over the "Lutyens elite" but he knows he has not and sees no reason why he should tolerate a long dead English architect's buildings.

In many ways his use of the term 'Lutyens elite' is shorthand for a battle that has been going on for many decades between urban India and rural India, big city versus small town, what Indians call moffusil towns, modern versus traditional, and English versus Indian languages. Even before Modi came to power smaller towns, once looked down by the elite, were gaining prominence.

Cricket, which is like a religion in India, exemplified this with the rise of Mahendra Singh Dhoni. Dhoni hails from Ranchi which in my youth was mocked as "pagla ghar" meaning mad house, a place where people with mental disease were sent to be looked after. Then it was inconceivable that it could be a place which could produce an Indian hero. Now, thanks to Dhoni, Ranchi has been so transformed that it ranks as a city, hosts international cricket matches and other events, and has the most modern airport in India. Modi's hometown, Vadnagar, is even lower down the scale than Ranchi and has only become known to most Indians because Modi was born there. The story of Ranchi is being repeated elsewhere in this vast land as smaller towns gain prominence and further marginalise the Lutyens elite.

Chapter 8

Modi the Missionary

One of Modi's great heroes is Swami Vivekananda. Like Patel he is hardly known outside India but his influence on India was colossal. A devotee of the Hindu monk, Ramakrishna, he had in the closing years of the 19th century, fashioned a liberal humanist Hinduism answering the British charge that such an idol-worshipping, caste-bound religion ought to be destroyed. He made his entrance on the international stage when at the World Parliament of Religions in Chicago on 11 September 1893 he electrified the audience. He had not prepared a speech, felt very nervous, did not know what to say and when asked to speak started by addressing the people gathered as "sisters and brothers of America".

It led to two minutes of deafening applause. He then explained Hinduism which many in that hall knew little about. He enraptured the audience, was hailed in the press and soon known all over America as the great Hindu monk. What makes this story even more extraordinary is that Vivekananda had arrived in America with only £188, lived on £1 a day, and a few days before he addressed the assembly had spent the night in an empty wagon at a railroad freight-yard.

He had even spent a morning along Chicago's affluent Lake Shore Drive knocking on doors for food but was turned away by the servants as his soiled clothes and unshaven face made him look a tramp. But then a kindly America woman took him in and with the President of the Assembly her personal friend

Vivekananda was provided the platform to make his historic address.

For Modi this story of his hero has great relevance. While Modi was not an unknown before he became Prime Minister, he was a pariah in a way no Indian seeking to be Prime Minister of India had ever been. The riots of Gujarat had cast such a shadow that he had been denied entry to America and there had been demands to stop him from coming to Britain.

Once elected however, America could not bar him and like Vivekananda he vowed a crowd at a sell-out rally in Madison Square Garden. Where Vivekananda had taught Americans what Hinduism was, Modi told them of the new India, that people in the land of the snake charmers now played with a computer mouse and that India had sent a spacecraft to Mars with a budget less than the Hollywood blockbuster *Gravity*. The *Times of India* described it as "a mutual love-fest that sharply etched the country's growing power and profile in the minds of Americans."

One difference with Vivekananda is noteworthy, that whereas in Chicago there were no Indian residents many of those at Madison Square Garden were people of Indian origin and Modi could praise the Indian Americans for what they had done for America. This resonated all the more with these Indians because, despite America claiming to welcome the world's poor, until the 1960s racist immigration laws prevented Indians, Chinese and other Asians from migrating to the US. The Indians Modi was addressing were the children of the Indians who had gone to America since John Kennedy and keen to advertise their status as Indian-Americans.

It was also significant that America was one of Modi's first foreign trips and in that he was following Vivekananda. When

Vivekananda went to America he did not follow the conventional Indian journey westwards, via the capital city of India's conquerors, London, before crossing the Atlantic. Instead, he headed east, via Colombo, Penang, Hong Kong, Canton, Nagasaki, Osaka, Kyoto, Tokyo, Yokohama and Vancouver.

The route was unprecedented then, and even nowadays, when many more Indians travel to the US, a Pacific routing rather than the Atlantic one is very rare. Vivekananda fell in love with America saying, "there is where the heart is. I love Yankee land." Modi has shown a similar liking for America and it was only after many trips to America that he came to Britain when in the past Indian Prime Ministers would have made Britain one of their first stops.

Courting America and the Indian Americans was part of Modi's calculation that he could build a strong Indian lobby in the most powerful country in the world. This was also the strategy he followed when he finally came to Britain holding a rally at Wembley where many people of Indian origin gathered, particularly from Gujarat. Watching the Indians gathering at Wembley there was no doubt that while the Indian football team would never be good enough to challenge England at Wembley, Modi could certainly draw a large Indian crowd.

The event also demonstrated how far Modi had come from his pariah day. Then Prime Minister David Cameron and his wife Samantha attended with Cameron speaking a few words in Gujarati and Samantha wearing a sari. Modi who has also cosied up to Benjamin Netanyahu, the Indian and Israeli leader even posing along a beach front, has clearly drawn lessons from how the Israeli government uses the Israel lobby in America, UK and other countries to influence policies in these countries.

In seeking to get close to America Modi was also seeking to correct what he sees as a fundamental flaw in Nehru's foreign policy. This had seen India, after becoming an independent nation, follow the non-aligned policy of keeping both the US and the Soviet Union at arms length during the Cold War. But underlying it was a deep distrust of America with Nehru saying, "I must say that the Americans, for all their great achievements, impress me less and less, so far as their human quality is concerned. They are apt to be more hysterical as a people than almost any others except perhaps the Bengalis. The Russians follow wrong courses often enough, but they remain calm and collected about it and do not show excitement."

Nehru disapproved of America's Asian policy of supporting every strong man who emerged provided he said he opposed communism. His daughter Indira had even more reason to distrust America. In 1971 as the Pakistani army led by west Pakistanis carried out a genocide in east Pakistan Richard Nixon sided with Pakistan's dictator Yahya Khan, as he was using him as a postman to open the door to China.

So determined was Nixon, who hated India and Indians, to stop India liberating east Pakistan and creating Bangladesh that he even sent the Seventh Fleet to the Bay of Bengal and proposed resolutions in the Security Council to halt India. America persuaded the UN General Assembly to ask India to pull back its troops although, unlike Security Council resolutions, this had no legal force. This has meant that in the Indian intellectual class there has always been much distrust of America.

Modi has tried hard to change this attitude and during the Trump Presidency worked diligently to get close to Trump. He was trying to build on the fact that in the 2016 elections Trump had courted Hindu voters in America .

Modi hoped Trump would make sure America would side with India, the calculation being that this would loosen American ties with Pakistan, a country America has bankrolled for decades and which India would like labelled a terrorist state. He also hoped that with China increasingly flexing its muscles should there be a clash with China Trump would stand by his friend Modi. However, Modi, like many world leaders, did not take into account how unpredictable Trump could be and when in 2020 it emerged that China had occupied a whole swathe of Indian territory Trump did not rush to Modi's aid. Nor has his courtship with Netanyahu yielded any dividends.

Chapter 9

Modi's Other Cycle

But what about Modi's other cycle, his business cycle? How well has he ridden it? The 2014 election saw him make much of the economic prosperity he had brought to Gujarat during his twelve-year rule. This had transformed Gujarat with the economy growing by 10.1 % between 2004 and 2012 when the national average was 7.6% and its contribution to the nation's industrial production was 16%, more than three times its population and while having only 6% of the land of the country.

In his early years in office, he certainly presented himself as the revolutionary who would take India on the path to progress . It is what many Indians like my friend Ajit has hoped for. "I have confidence that the man will change India and for the better. He is going to bring a lot of order to this society."

Modi certainly started off by behaving like no other Indian Prime Minister had done. In his very first speech in May 2014 on the day he won power, while promising to do his best for India, he asked the citizens of Varansi, one of two constituencies he had won(it is common to contest two seats in Indian elections) to help him by cleaning up their city. Indian Prime Ministers do not talk about the filth that can make walking Indian streets such an unpleasant experience. But Modi was keen to talk to Indians about the dirt amidst which they lived.

In his first Independence Day speech from the Red Fort on 15 August he made history by becoming the first Indian Prime

Minister to address the issue of toilets. He announced a £20 billion "Clean India" campaign with plans to train 50,000 people, each of whom was to construct 3,000 lavatories over the next five years, and see 110 million lavatories constructed, the biggest construction of lavatories the world has ever seen.

His hope was that by 2019 no Indian would defecate publicly. This was held out as a wonderful birthday present for the Mahatma, as 2019 marked the 150th anniversary of his birth. The Mahatma had spoken at length about how Indians needed to learn cleanliness and given detailed instructions as to how they should use a latrine.

But like Gandhi Modi has not found it easy to change age old Indian habits. After the Clean India campaign constructed more than half a million household latrines, mostly in the improvised rural interior, Modi had to appoint an army of inspectors to check whether the state-built lavatories in homes around the country were being used for the purpose for which they were intended.

The sanitary inspectors made house-to-house calls to "check and verify the use of toilets" uploading the information to the database using mobile phones and tablets. They found that they had been converted for other uses, such as storerooms and sheds. The reason was many Indians prefer to defecate in the open, believing household toilets are a source of pollution and impurity. The Hindus were most reluctant - 47 per cent of Hindu homes have no toilets, as opposed to 31 per cent of Muslim homes and 16 per cent of Christian and Sikh homes. When asked by academics from Princeton University the reasons given for preferring to defecate in the open varied from "pleasurable, comfortable or convenient" to "provides them with an opportunity to take a morning walk, see their fields and take in the fresh air", and that it was part of a "wholesome, healthy, virtuous life."

The survey also found that in 18 per cent of Indian households where a lavatory had been installed, at least one family member opted to continue defecating outside – usually men, who often expressed a clear preference.

If such ingrained Indian habits are difficult to change, the early years of the Modi Raj certainly suggested he would get a Gujarat style growth in India. India's economic growth rocketed from 6.4 % in 2013 to a high of 7.9% in 2015 making India the fasted growing economy in the world. He overhauled the bankruptcy laws, adopted a national sales tax which replaced the often confusing medley of local taxes and national levies. India attracted foreign investment on a scale it had not before.

Modi was also made much of the fact that he would make sure India's vast army of bureaucrats, what Indians call "babus", actually worked, came to their offices in time and did not take long lunch hours. Yet as events since have shown Modi far from proving to a revolutionary has turned out to be more of a tinkerer. Worse still in a country where decision making at government level can be very slow Modi's bold moves have often proved not well thought out and led to disastrous consequences.

Successive Indian leaders have talked about dealing with the black economy and failed. So widespread is the black economy that when it comes to buying and selling homes the property dealer will ask "How much white, how much black?". This means part of the purchase price will be paid in cash by the vendor drawing on money on which tax has not been paid. This also means the price of the house as shown in official records is less than its real price reducing the tax burden on the owner.

Modi's answer to dealing with the black economy was to demonetise the currency. The 500 rupee and the 1000 rupee notes in circulation were declared as no longer valid currency. They were replaced by new notes. But this was announced with so little planning and with such suddenness that it caused untold problems for millions of India. Indians suddenly found they had no cash, and this even caused deaths as some people were not able to get any cash.

His response to the Coronavirus also showed how little thought goes into decision making. With dramatic suddenness India was shut down. People were banned from leaving their homes for three weeks under the "total lockdown" measures. All non-essential businesses were closed and almost all public gatherings were banned.

No thought was given to the thousands of migrant workers who work in the big cities of India. Tens of thousands of migrant labourers were forced to walk hundreds of kilometres to their native villages. Some of them never made it dying along the way.

The disaster forced Modi in his weekly radio address to apologise, "Especially when I look at my poor brothers and sisters, I definitely feel that they must be thinking, what kind of prime minister is this who has placed us in this difficulty? I especially seek their forgiveness. Possibly many would be angry at me for being locked in their homes." But justified it on the grounds that, "I understand your troubles but there was no other way to wage war against coronavirus... It is a battle of life and death and we have to win it."

Despite such measures India soon had the second highest number of cases after the United States and Indians could see the sharp contrast in how Modi had handled the crisis compared to the efficiency of east Asian countries like Korea. Modi's India would like to match what these countries have done to lift their people out of poverty and the pandemic response showed how far India is still lagging behind.

The pandemic has also seen India take the unwanted prize for worst effected of the major economies. In the April-June quarter of 2020 the Indian gross domestic product shrank by 23.9%—the worst contraction ever in India's history. With the economy also shrinking in the following quarter India entered its first economic recession since the British left in 1947.

The Modi government was quick to comfort Indians by saying that there would be, as finance minister Nirmala Sitharaman put it, a "V-shaped recovery." But that seems very optimistic. 2020 has seen per capita GDP fall by 11%, making Indians on an average poorer than Bangladeshis.

There are various economic forecasts on how India will fare.

The IMF has predicted that only at the end of 2022 per capita GDP will be back at pre-Covid-19 levels. But this does not take into account inflation or, of course, how much the economy might have risen had there been no pandemic. A gloomier forecast is provided by Sabyasachi Kar, who holds the Reserve Bank of India Chair at the National Institute of Public Finance and Policy. He predicts that it will take India up to 2033 to get back on the pre-Covid growth path. Even that assumes GDP grows at 7% for the next 13 years. Economic forecasts are always what if scenarios and should growth rate be 6.1%, which it was in 2018-2019, then India would have to wait until 2049 to get back on the pre-Covid-19 growth path. And even

6.1% over such a long period is being very optimistic given that India averaged a growth of 5.5% in the 1990s and early 2000s.

Chapter 10

The 56-inch Teflon Man

Yet despite all this there is no evidence that Modi's own stock has fallen. Modi in one of his speeches boasted he had a 56-inch chest and while this has often been mocked by his political opponents his supporters see this as just the chest a strong man would have. In that sense he is the ultimate Teflon man.

His policies may cause enormous problems, but his personal standing is not affected. I had a vivid illustration of this when I visited India soon after the disastrous monetisation. Indians complained about the impact it had had but few blamed Modi for it. He seemed above it all. Indians seem to think he is different to other Indian politicians. In a country where corruption is endemic and nepotism the rule with politicians making politics a family business, a father is succeeded by his son or daughter or even at times by his wife, as the Nehrus have done for generations, Modi stands apart.

As Ajit Gulabchand put it, "I believe Narendra Modi is a very sincere man and a man of high integrity. He is not corrupt. His family is not involved in politics. He has told his wife she must stand on her own feet. He meets his mother once a year on his birthday. His brothers have nothing to do with him. He is spiritual in nature, having spent a few years in the Himalayas."

Modi's ability to ride out bad government policies may also be because his rule has not been subject to sharp media analysis. One journalist I spoke to, who works for one of India's leading papers, told me, "What Modi and his government is doing is micromanaging the media, government by headline. There is hardly any journalism happening now. Modi's government has cowed the media." What was really revealing was when I asked him whether I could name him and his newspaper he said, "No, no please do not." In 2017, three years into Modi's rule, Arun Shourie, a former BJP minister, caused a great deal of controversy when he compared the Indian media to the North Korean media.

While he may have been over dramatizing it, Indian media has certainly been reluctant to criticise Modi and his government with Indian newspaper barons keen to make sure they are on the right side. They are aware that the government can use its massive advertising budget to target newspapers which it favours.

The government's reaction to the media coverage of the farmers agitation shows how it can use state power, even laws inherited from the British Raj and used by the colonial regime to curb dissent, to strike against the media. The media coverage of the farmers protest in Delhi on 26 January, 2021 led to government authorities issuing what are called First Information Reports, the first step in criminal prosecution, against leading editors and journalists for their coverage of the event. It resulted in a strong protest from the Commonwealth Journalists Association which called "on the Indian Government to honour its international commitments to the Commonwealth and to the UN and ensure that the media is free to play its constitutional role as a guardian of the public interest and in holding elected governments to account."

But such criticism will not worry Modi. The farmers protest had come on India's Republic Day, which celebrates the day India became a republic. It is a more important date than August 15, as that marks the day when India got Dominion Status but the British monarch was still technically the head of state of India. In contrast, Republic Day marks the moment when India got its own constitution, electing its own President, and is seen as the moment it truly emerged as a free nation.

Modi's government could present the farmers' protest that day as an act of sedition and, just as the Raj did, journalists who covered it were also considered seditious. Modi and his supporters were confident that much of the country, which in any case has a low opinion of the Indian media, would support the action.

What is of greater significance for Modi and his government is that such actions has meant that India, which has always had a raucous media which lives and breathes politics, now often lets much of what Modi's Raj does go by without too much scrutiny.

Not that this makes Modi completely in charge of India in the way Nehru and for a time his daughter Indira Gandhi was. The BJP has expanded beyond its traditional Hindi heartland of northern and central India to states like Bengal in the east which is remarkable.

This was a state where for more than thirty years Indian communists were in power and a party associated with Hindu fundamentalism stood no chance of getting power. Now the BJP is close to winning the forthcoming state elections. However, many parts of the south still remain out of reach for the party.

But where Modi has outmatched Nehru is that he is just the strong man that many in India have always wanted. In the 60s as Nehru nurtured India's democracy there was much debate as to whether India would be better off with a leader like Kemal Ataturk of Turkey.

The argument was that democracy was a talking shop but did not provide scope for the quick, dramatic, changes a poor country needed. But in the end the conclusion was that Nehru was the best leader India could have and the democratic roots he was planting would thrive and prosper. Modi now seems more like an Indian Ataturk. But this does not mean India could become like Turkey.

Unlike Turkey, India is a very diverse country with various political forces at work at state levels all over the country which means there will always be a challenge to Modi's BJP. Unlike in the early years of the Indian republic when the Congress was the only party, now there are many strong regional parties, one party dominating all of India seems impossible.

And Indian democracy has always shown great resilience.

In 1975 Indira Gandhi, then the almighty leader in the mould of Modi, fearful of losing power, declared a state of emergency, the nearest India since independence has come to becoming a dictatorship. Opposition leaders were jailed and Modi, fearing arrest, was forced into hiding. "Indira is India" was the slogan of her followers. It seemed democracy would never revive in India and many foreign politicians including Michael Foot supported what Mrs Gandhi was doing.

But three years later when Mrs Gandhi held elections the voters repudiated her, Mrs Gandhi herself lost her seat, and India returned to democratic ways. A little more than a decade later the socialism that Mrs Gandhi had made into an article of faith had been abandoned for a free market philosophy.

So, while Modi's rule is changing India and all the signs are of India being transformed from a secular republic to more of a Hindu Raj, the Indian capacity to change direction with no notice and follow a completely different tack can never be ruled out. Modi's story itself illustrates that. Many even in his party did not think this tea seller could be a Prime Minister who could possibly lead India. But he did, illustrating India's capacity for embracing sudden change, and it is very difficult to predict the new direction. Or who may emerge to lead this remarkable, maddening, bewildering but, always, fascinating country.

BITE-SIZED BOOKS

Bite-Sized Public Affairs Books are designed to provide insights and stimulating ideas that affect us all in, for example, journalism, social policy, education, government and politics.

They are deliberately short, easy to read, and authoritative books written by people who are either on the front line or who are informed observers. They are designed to stimulate discussion, thought and innovation in all areas of public affairs. They are all firmly based on personal experience and direct involvement and engagement.

The most successful people all share an ability to focus on what really matters, keeping things simple and understandable. When we are faced with a new challenge most of us need quick guidance on what matters most, from people who have been there before and who can show us where to start.

They can be read straight through at one easy sitting and then referred to as necessary – a trusted repository of hard-won experience.

BITE-SIZED BOOKS

Catalogue

Bite-Sized Books cover business, public affairs, lifestyle, fiction and children's fiction. The full catalogue can be found at:

https://bite-sizedbooks.com/product-category/all/

Printed in Great Britain
by Amazon